© for the Spanish edition: 2018, Mosquito Books, Barcelona
www.mosquitobooksbarcelona.com
© for the illustrations: 2018, Marcos Navarro
© for the text: 2018, Mia Cassany
© for the English edition: 2019, Prestel Verlag, Munich · London · New York
A member of Verlagsgruppe Random House GmbH
Neumarkter Strasse 28 · 81673 Munich

Prestel Publishing Ltd.
14-17 Wells Street
London, W1T 3PD

Prestel Publishing
900 Broadway, Suite 603
New York, NY 10003

In respect to links in the book, the Publisher expressly notes that no illegal content was discernible on the linked sites at the time the links were created. The Publisher has no influence at all over the current and future design, content or authorship of the linked sites. For this reason the Publisher expressly disassociates itself from all content on linked sites that has been altered since the link was created and assumes no liability for such content.

Library of Congress Control Number: 2018949221
A CIP catalogue record for this book is available from the British Library.

Translated from German by Paul Kelly
Copyediting: John Son
Project management: Melanie Schöni
Production management: Astrid Wedemeyer
Typesetting: Wolfram Söll, designwerk
Printing and binding: DZS Grafik d.o.o.
Paper: Tauro

Verlagsgruppe Random House FSC® N001967
Printed in Slovenia

ISBN 978-3-7913-7372-0
www.prestel.com

WILDERNESS

EARTH'S AMAZING HABITATS

MIA CASSANY · MARCOS NAVARRO

PRESTEL
Munich · London · New York

THE HABITATS OF RARE ANIMALS AND PLANTS

Earth's wildernesses represent true paradises for many plants and animals. These wild landscapes cover only about 5% of the Earth's surface, yet they are home to roughly half of the plant and animal species we know at this time. And new species are constantly being discovered!

As the habitats of rare plants and animals, these wildernesses need our protection. But they are shrinking every day: deforestation is increasing at an alarming rate, which greatly impacts climate change. Human intervention is leading to the disappearance of many habitats and species.

On the following pages, you will get to know some of the most amazing landscapes on Earth. Each one of these is unique and worthy of preservation.

Like nature, everything portrayed in this book is vivid and buzzing with life. Everything breathes: from a tiny chick that moves inside its egg to the powerful tiger that roams the Forest, from the enormous roots of thousand-year-old trees to their gloriously vibrant blossoms. Explore these mysterious and exciting worlds. Observe monkeys in the treetops, spiders in their webs, frogs in the vegetation, and so much more.

Welcome to the most stunning nature show on Earth!

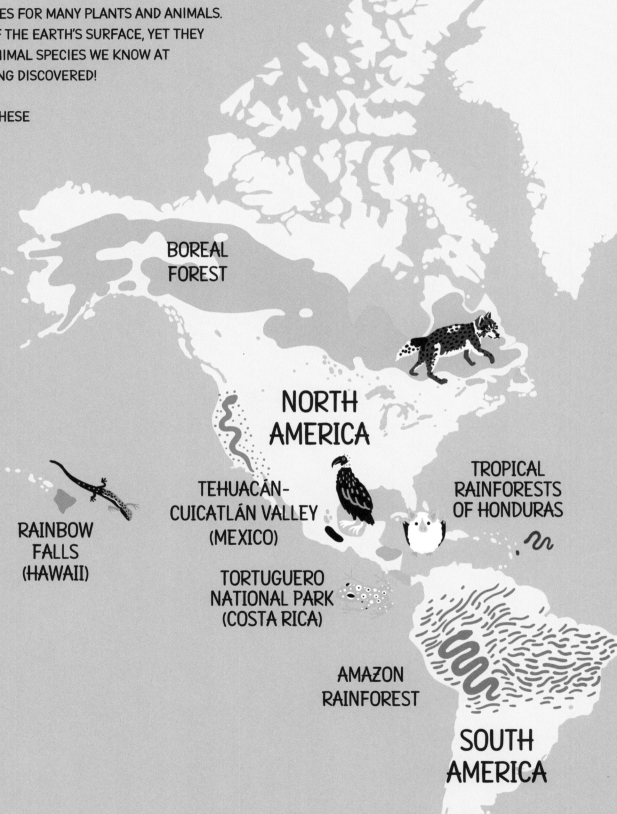

BOREAL FOREST

NORTH AMERICA

RAINBOW FALLS (HAWAII)

TEHUACÁN-CUICATLÁN VALLEY (MEXICO)

TROPICAL RAINFORESTS OF HONDURAS

TORTUGUERO NATIONAL PARK (COSTA RICA)

AMAZON RAINFOREST

SOUTH AMERICA

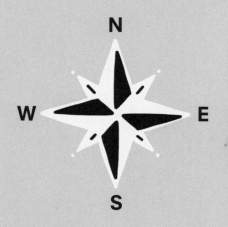

N
W **E**
S

ASIA

SIKHOTE-ALIN NATURE
RESERVE (RUSSIA)

EUROPE

QINLING MOUNTAINS
(CHINA)

SUNDARBANS
NATIONAL PARK (INDIA)

TROPICAL RAINFORESTS OF
SOUTHEAST ASIA (MALAYSIA)

TROPICAL
RAINFOREST OF
NEW GUINEA

AFRICA

NIOKOLO-KOBA
NATIONAL PARK
(SENEGAL)

KAHUZI-BIÉGA
NATIONAL PARK
(CONGO)

SINHARAJA FOREST
RESERVE
(SRI LANKA)

DAINTREE
NATIONAL
PARK

AUSTRALIA

TROPICAL
RAINFOREST OF
MADAGASCAR

NIOKOLO-KOBA NATIONAL PARK

Located in the southeast corner of Africa's Senegal, this national park is a UNESCO World Heritage Site.
This means it has been singled out to be protected for future generations. Safeguarding such regions is
a global matter because there are flora (plants) and fauna (animals) living here that are unique to our planet.

Niokolo-Koba and the full length of the river Gambia are home to a great number of wild animals, such as
leopards, baboons, elephants, lions, and hippos, many of which are endangered or have already been killed due
to poaching, or in other words, illegal hunting. Even the construction of a planned dam represents a threat.
This is why the park is under special protection.

KAHUZI-BIÉGA NATIONAL PARK

The national park of Kahuzi-Biéga is located in the Democratic Republic of Congo in Central Africa. Named after two extinct volcanoes, the Kahuzi and the Biéga, the park consists of a huge tropical rainforest containing over 200 native species. The area was declared a World Heritage Site in 1980 due to tribal warfare and poaching. It is home to the last surviving group of eastern lowland gorillas—the largest species of gorilla.

QINLING MOUNTAINS

Qinling is the name of the largest chain of mountains in Shaanxi Province, right in the middle of China. These mountainous forests are home to a variety of rare plants and animals, including the Qinling panda, of which there are only about 250 left. Unlike their larger giant panda cousins, the fur of Qinling pandas are light and dark brown in color. There is no other place on earth where these brown pandas can be found, and they are protected because of their rarity.

SUNDARBANS NATIONAL PARK

India's Sundarbans National Park is made up of 54 small islands, with seven rivers and countless waterways forming a network of canals that flow into the sea.

The park is densely covered by mangrove forests made up of trees and shrubs that have adapted their roots to life between saltwater and fresh water. This makes an ideal home for endangered land and marine animals. More than 400 Bengal tigers live here, along with saltwater crocodiles and numerous types of birds and fish.

SIKHOTE-ALIN NATURE RESERVE

This massive nature reserve is located in the far east of Russia and stretches out as far as the Sea of Japan. Thanks to its unusually diverse climate, a mix between taiga and subtropical, it is home to species that aren't usually found together, like the Himalayan bear and the brown bear. It is also the habitat of unique mammals like the Amur tiger, Siberian musk deer, wolverine, and sable.

TROPICAL RAINFORESTS OF SOUTHEAST ASIA

The tropical rainforests of Malaysia in Southeast Asia are among the oldest in the world. Scientists estimate they are over 100 million years old. They harbor a multitude of insects that are able to adapt and survive in a wide variety of climates. Butterflies and moths are the best examples of this versatility. The flamboyantly patterned creatures have a very important role to play when it comes to the cycle of nature: they carry pollen from one flower to the next, ensuring that new life continues to be created.

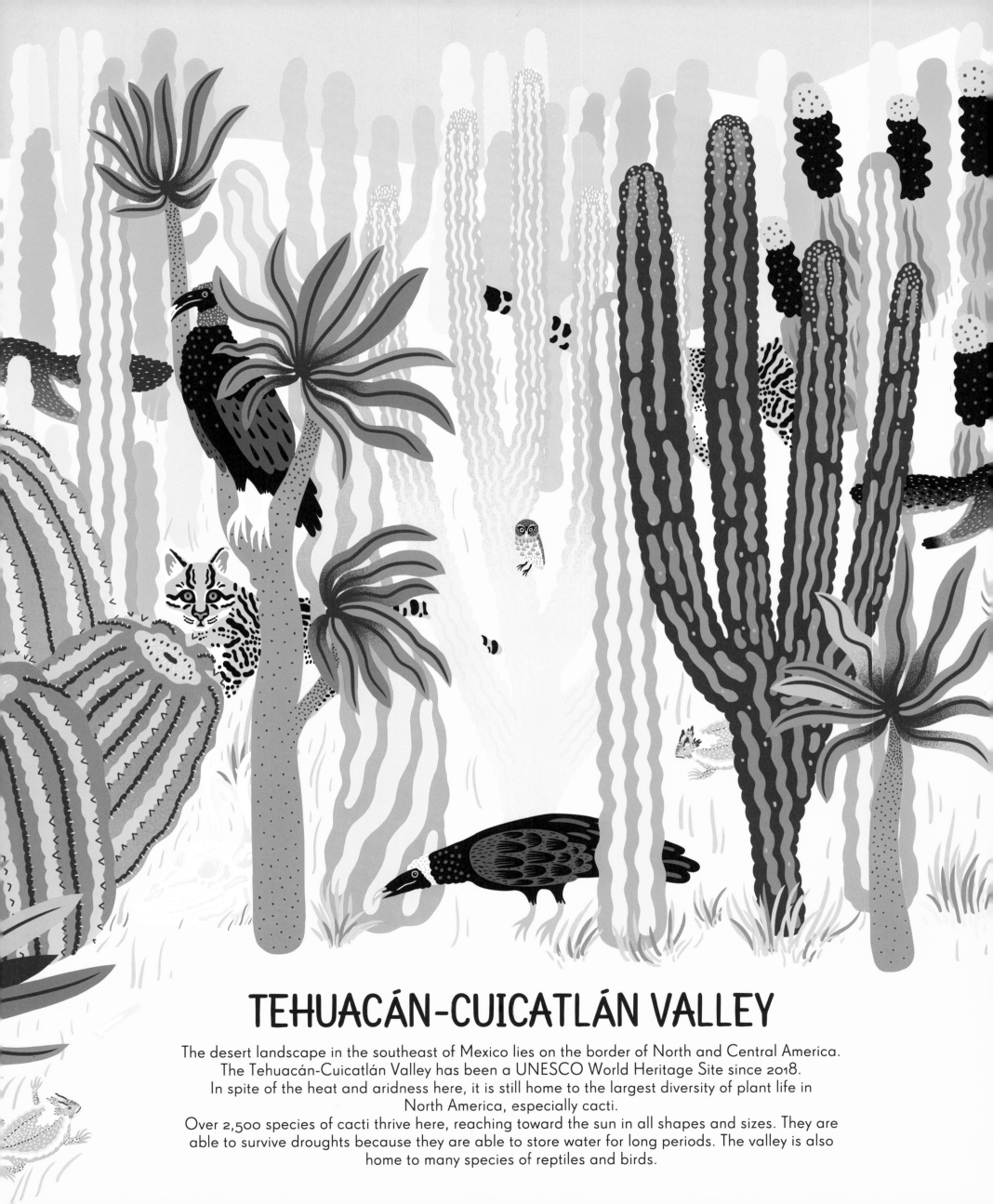

TEHUACÁN-CUICATLÁN VALLEY

The desert landscape in the southeast of Mexico lies on the border of North and Central America. The Tehuacán-Cuicatlán Valley has been a UNESCO World Heritage Site since 2018. In spite of the heat and aridness here, it is still home to the largest diversity of plant life in North America, especially cacti.

Over 2,500 species of cacti thrive here, reaching toward the sun in all shapes and sizes. They are able to survive droughts because they are able to store water for long periods. The valley is also home to many species of reptiles and birds.

TROPICAL RAINFORESTS OF MADAGASCAR

The island of Madagascar became detached from the African mainland over 150 million years ago. Cut off from Africa, a unique and diverse range of animals and plants evolved, including lemurs and nearly 300 species of frogs. Great numbers of geckos also hide in the rainforests. The island's health is under very serious threat from human settlement, hunting, cattle farming, and deforestation.

Before humans came to the island, even more unusual animals used to live here, such as giant lemurs, which were as big as orangutans, and the elephant bird and Malagasy hippopotamus.

SINHARAJA FOREST RESERVE

The unspoiled tropical forest of Sinharaja is found on the island of Sri Lanka. An abundance
of animals chirp, twitter, and growl in its dense vegetation.
The rainforest's natural density has helped protect it from deforestation. It is almost impossible for
humans to enter its wilderness, which includes hundreds of rare and native plants and trees.
The reserve is also home to many rare and endangered animal species, like the purple-faced langur,
the brown-patched kangaroo lizard, and the long-nosed whip snake.

TORTUGUERO
NATIONAL PARK

Tortuguero National Park owes its name to turtles, called *tortugas* in Spanish. Many endangered sea turtles lay their eggs on the Caribbean beaches of Costa Rica. Among these is the green sea turtle.

Costa Rica is one of the rainiest areas in the world. Many trees have evolved gigantic leaves that provide shelter to the park's animals, including its many exotic frogs.

BOREAL FOREST

The boreal forest—also known as taiga—is the largest forested expanse on earth. This wilderness stretches from the north of Canada through Alaska and Russia. It is the northernmost nature reserve in the world.

The average temperature is 66°F (19°C) in summer and in winter it can drop down to -22°F (-30°C)! Pines and fir trees have adapted to these harsh conditions perfectly well. Thanks to their sharp needles, these trees are very frost resistant. Elk, moose, porcupine, lynx, fox, and coyote are just some of the many species that live among the trees.

RAINBOW FALLS

In the middle of a lush rainforest on the island of Hawaii, the Wailuku
River plunges down into a very large basin over a natural lava cave. Water
shimmers in a shade of turquoise and is surrounded by wild vegetation.
It's a tropical paradise that's also home to many colorful animal species.
On sunny mornings, the mist from the waterfall creates beautiful rainbows,
giving this paradise its name.

AMAZON RAINFOREST

In South America you can find the largest tropical forest in the world. The whole region stretches across nine different countries. This seemingly endless world of trees and plants consists mainly of palm trees, lianas, and epiphytes, which are plants that grow on top of other plants. The dense rain forest is the perfect hiding place for hundreds of different snake species, which come in all sorts of colors and sizes.

TROPICAL RAINFORESTS OF HONDURAS

The Central American country of Honduras is covered in colorful rainforests. The forest to the north is evergreen. Its plants maintain their leaves all year long. Like the Amazon, the rainforests of Honduras are also dense with epiphytes. There are also at least 630 types of orchids, which are highly prized by collectors around the world. Hundreds of bright birds like toucans and scarlet macaws flit between the dense vegetation, as well as many species of bats and monkeys.

TROPICAL RAINFOREST OF NEW GUINEA

The tropical rainforest of New Guinea is the habitat of
almost 800 species of birds.
The colorfully feathered birds-of-paradise decorate the national flag of
New Guinea. The largest bird of this rainforest is the cassowary, a relative
of the emu in Australia. Like the emu and ostrich, cassowary can't fly.
Instead they run on very strong legs that have very sharp claws.
The tropical rainforest of New Guinea is one of the most untouched
wildernesses in the world. An incredibly rich mix of flora and fauna thrives
on this true treasure of an island.

DAINTREE NATIONAL PARK

This unique national park in Queensland, Australia, was declared a UNESCO
World Heritage Site in 1988.
The large rainforest of Daintree is a primeval wilderness that has not been disturbed by
humankind. At over 100 million years old, Daintree is one of the oldest rainforests on
the planet. Lianas grow undisturbed on the coast, their woody vines seeming to reach up
to the clouds. Mangrove forests hug the ancient Daintree River. Many of Daintree
National Park's giant trees are over 3,000 years old.

WOULD YOU LIKE TO FIND OUT MORE?

Animal name | 🔍 Number of animals on the page | More information on some of the animals

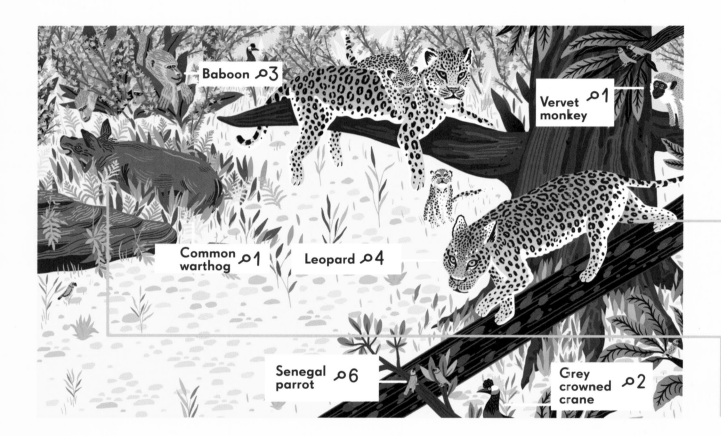

Baboon 🔍3

Vervet monkey 🔍1

Common warthog 🔍1

Leopard 🔍4

Senegal parrot 🔍6

Grey crowned crane 🔍2

Leopard:
The leopard is a mammal from the "big cat" family. They are powerful hunters who feed at night and rest during the day, often on tree branches as they are skilled climbers. One of the fastest animals in the world, leopards can run 36 mph (59 km/h)!

Warthog
Warthogs are quite common throughout Africa. They have sharp tusks and bumps (warts) on their head to protect themselves. Part of the pig family, these grazers like to make homes in the abandoned dens of aardvarks.

Eastern lowland gorilla:
Like all gorillas, the largest member of the gorilla family is a herbivore. A male can eat up to 40 pounds (18 kg) of leaves, fruits, stems, and bark a day. They get most of their water from the plants they eat. They are gentle, social creatures who spend their days resting, feeding, and socializing in families of up to 30 members.

Eurasian scops owl 🔍1

African palm squirrel 🔍3

African forest buffalo 🔍2

Eastern lowland gorilla 🔍10

Yellow-crested helmetshrike 🔍4

Peacock 🔍1

Green-banded swallowtail 🔍5

Golden takin:
Also called goat-antelope, golden takin make their home in the mountains.

Black-throated robin 🔎 4

Qinling panda 🔎 1

Golden snub-nosed monkey 🔎 5

Golden takin 🔎 1

Golden pheasant 🔎 3

Golden pheasant:
The males of this species show off their vibrant feathers to attract females. Otherwise, these clumsy fliers spend most of their time on the ground, hiding in the woods.

Qinling panda:
A member of the bear family, pandas only eat bamboo, but because bamboo is low in nutrients, they have to eat large quantities. Sometimes they spend 12 hours a day eating!

Bengal tiger:
The Bengal tiger has the unique talent of being able to swim in saltwater. These animals can be seen on the riverbank from November to February, when they are soaking up the sun.

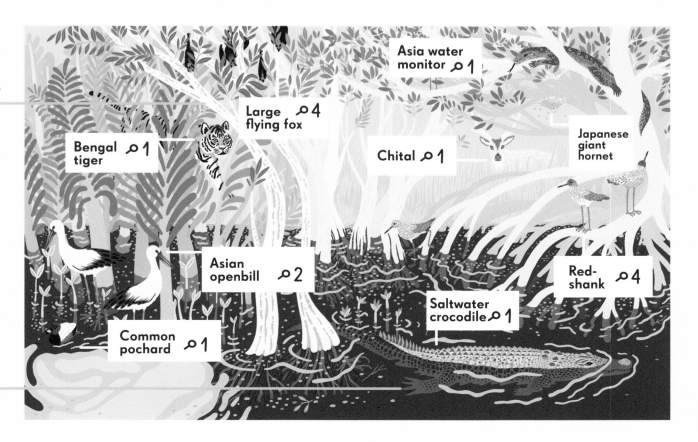

Asia water monitor 🔎 1

Large flying fox 🔎 4

Bengal tiger 🔎 1

Chital 🔎 1

Japanese giant hornet

Asian openbill 🔎 2

Red-shank 🔎 4

Saltwater crocodile 🔎 1

Common pochard 🔎 1

Saltwater crocodile:
The world's largest crocodile (and reptile) also has the strongest bite in the world. Though they can weigh over 1,000 pounds (453 kg), they can attack their prey in the blink of an eye.

Blakiston's fish owl 1

Snake 1

Elk 2

Wild boar 1

Hare 1

Pika 2

Siberian musk deer 1

Siberian tiger 1

Mayfly 3

Siberian tiger:
The Siberian tiger is the largest of the predator cats in the world. Its fur gets thicker and longer in the winter. At short distances, it can reach great speeds on the icy surfaces of the Siberian forests. The solitary predator travels long distances to catch its prey, which includes wild boar and reindeer

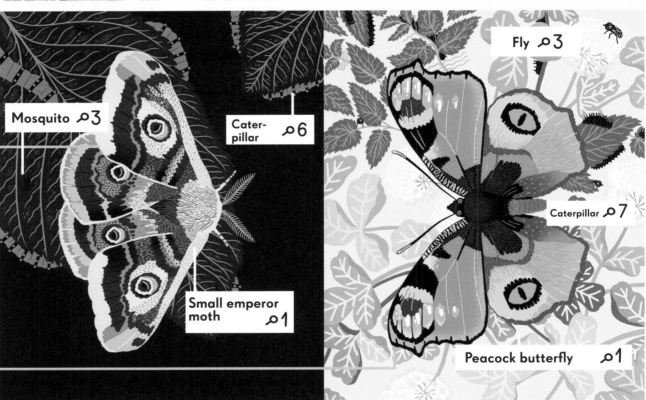

Moths:
Moths use the moon and stars to find their way at night. They are also important pollinators.

Butterflies:
Butterflies are insects. Most live for about a week, but a few species can live up to several months. Their wings are actually transparent and covered in tiny scales that reflect different colors of light, creating the beautiful patterns on their wings.

Mosquito 3

Caterpillar 6

Small emperor moth 1

Fly 3

Caterpillar 7

Peacock butterfly 1

Black vulture 8

Pygmy owl 2

South American gray fox 2

Ocelot 3

Horned lizard 2

Ocelot:
About twice the size of a domestic cat, ocelots are nocturnal carnivores that travel up to five miles at night, hunting prey like rodents, young deer, and snakes. During the day, they sleep in trees and bushes.

Black vulture:
This scavenger has a wingspan of over 5 feet (1.5 m).

Geckos:

Geckos are part of the scaly reptile family. Most are insectivores, but there are some that feed on fruit, small mammals, and on other reptiles. They can cling on to almost any surface just with their feet. They are great climbers and live mainly in trees.

Satanic leaf-tailed gecko 🔎 3

Firebug 🔎 2

Giraffe weevil 🔎 4

Ladybug 🔎 4

Millipede 🔎 1

Stick bug 🔎 1

Eggs 🔎 9

Madagascan moon moth 🔎 3

Swallowtail filter 🔎 3

Sri Lanka white-eye 🔎 7

White-headed langur 🔎 2

Toque macaque 🔎 7

Calotes 🔎 3

Sri Lanka blue magpie 🔎 6

Purple-faced langur 🔎 2

Flying snake 🔎 1

Toque macaque

Native to Sri Lanka, this primate gets its name from the hat-like crop of hair on its head. Not only does it have an unusually long tail, they have powerful jaws and cheek pouches that can hold as much food as their stomachs.

Glass frog:

The skin on a glass frog's belly is translucent, which means you can see its heart and intestines through the skin. They are also arboreal animals, which means they spend their lives in trees.

Ants 🔎 12

Glass frog 🔎 1

Long-horned grasshoppers 🔎 2

Frog-spawn

Wasp 🔎 1

Reindeer 1

Raccoon 3

Canada lynx 1

Snowshoe hare 2

Canada warbler 7

Mourning warbler 7

Black-backed woodpec- 2

American marten 2

Wolf 6

Ruffed Grouse 2

Wolves:
Even though wolves are portrayed in fairytales as evil and dangerous, they are in truth timid and suspicious. They shy away from people and only attack when they feel threatened.

Howling:
Stories often tell how wolves howl at the moon. In reality, they howl in order to communicate, to announce their location, to mark their territory and to assemble the pack. Wolves are often seen together at night because the moonlight improves their vision and makes for more successful hunting.

American marten:
Martens are nocturnal omnivores that eat mice, squirrels, fruit, and nuts. Although they look quite cuddly, they are in fact fierce predators with sharp teeth.

Reindeer:
Male reindeer lose their mighty antlers at the end of winter but they start to grow back a short while later. Females wear their antlers throughout the whole year

San Francisco garter snake:
This garter snake is one of the most magnificent and beautiful snakes in the world. Even though this slippery creature is able to hide very well, it is still threatened with extinction.

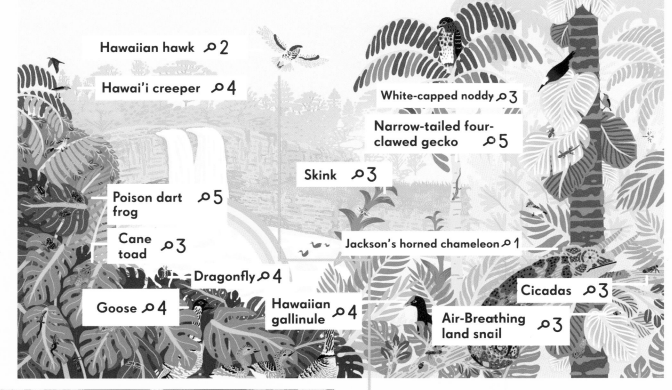

Hawaiian hawk 2

Hawai'i creeper 4

White-capped noddy 3

Narrow-tailed four-clawed gecko 5

Skink 3

Poison dart frog 5

Cane toad 3

Jackson's horned chameleon 1

Dragonfly 4

Goose 4

Hawaiian gallinule 4

Cicadas 3

Air-Breathing land snail 3

Giant anaconda 1

Darkling beetle 1

San Francisco garter snake 1

Barbados threadsnake 2

Hawaiian hawk:
Hawks are among the fastest birds on earth. When they dive for prey, they can fly up to 150 mph (241 kmh). Their vision is eight times better than humans, which allows them to hunt from great heights.

Giant anaconda:
The giant anaconda comes from the boa family of snakes and is in fact the largest snake species in the world. They can grow up to 16 feet (5 m) long. These constrictors hunt for their prey near river banks, swallowing them whole once they have been squeezed to death.

Barbados threadsnake:
The smallest snake species is only 4 inches (10cm) long and feeds on small insects like ants and termites.

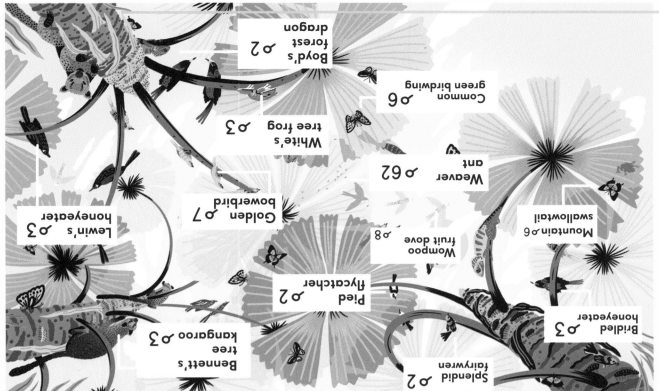

Bennett's tree kangaroo:
This endangered marsupial is closely related to the kangaroo but lives in trees. This beautiful animal with strong shiny fur and yellow stripes running down its back is about as big as a fully grown hare. Like all marsupials, it sleeps about 12 hours a day.

Boyd's forest dragon ♂2

Common green birdwing ♂6

White's tree frog ♂3

Weaver ant ♂62

Golden bowerbird ♂7

Lewin's honeyeater ♂3

Wompoo fruit dove ♂8

Mountain ♂6 swallowtail

Pied flycatcher ♂2

Bridled honeyeater ♂3

Bennett's tree kangaroo ♂3

Splendid fairywren ♂2

Blue bird-of-paradise:
Birds-of-paradise are renowned for their astounding plumage. Depending on the angle, different shades of light and color are reflected by the feathers. And because of this spectacular effect, the birds are said to have magical powers.

Snout Beetle (Eupholus tupinerii) ♂4

Jewel Beetle ♂3

Blue bird-of-paradise ♂6

Stag beetle ♂2

Dragonfly ♂3

Eupholus bennetti beetle ♂2

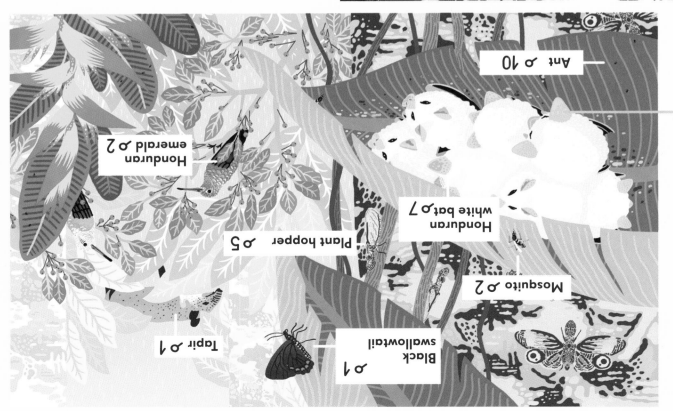

Honduran white bat:
Snow white with a yellow nose and yellow ears, the Honduran white bat is the smallest known bat. During the day, these nocturnal creatures build nests under the leaves of Heliconia flowering plants, where they huddle in groups of six or more bats for protection.

Ant ♂10

Honduran emerald ♂2

Honduran white bat ♂7

Plant hopper ♂5

Mosquito ♂2

Tapir ♂1

Black swallowtail ♂1